My Favourite Dogs

LABRADOR RETRIEVER

Jinny Johnson

FRANKLIN WATTS
LONDON•SYDNEY

 An Appleseed Editions book

First published in 2013 by Franklin Watts
338 Euston Road, London NW1 3BH

© 2012 Appleseed Editions

Created by Appleseed Editions Ltd,
Well House, Friars Hill, Guestling,
East Sussex TN35 4ET

Designed and illustrated by Hel James
Edited by Mary-Jane Wilkins

ISBN 978 1 4451 2179 6

Dewey Classification: 636.7'527

A CIP catalogue for this book is available from the British Library.

Photo acknowledgements
t = top, b = bottom
page 1 Tina Rencelj/Shutterstock; 3 c.byatt-norman/Shutterstock; 4 Gorilla/Shutterstock;
5 Pawel Cebo/Shutterstock; 6 iStockphoto/Thinkstock; 7 Gerald Marella/Shutterstock;
8-9 Erik Lam/Shutterstock;
10-11 Teresa Kasprzycka/Shutterstock; 12 iStockphoto/Thinkstock;
13t Ryan McVay/Thinkstock, b ARENA Creative/Shutterstock;
14 iStockphoto/Thinkstock; 15 karam Miri/Shutterstock;
16-17 Vlad Ageshin/Shutterstock; 18 Hemera/Thinkstock;
19 Huntstock/Thinkstock; 20 Tatiana Gass/Shutterstock;
21 aspen rock Shutterstock; 23 Gorilla/Shutterstock
Cover Eric Isselée/Shutterstock

Printed in China

Franklin Watts is a division of Hachette Children's Books,
an Hachette UK company.
www.hachette.co.uk

Contents

I'm a Labrador retriever! 4

What I need 6

The Labrador retriever 8

All about Labrador retrievers 10

Growing up 12

Training your dog 14

Water dogs 16

Working dogs 18

Your healthy dog 20

Caring for your dog 22

Useful words 24

Index 24

I'm a Labrador retriever!

I'm a big softie. I'm lovable, brave and loyal and I'll do anything for my family. I love to help and I love to please. I'm good with children, too.

What I need

I like to work hard and play hard, and I need a good walk every day. I'm happy running alongside when my owner goes for a run or a bike ride. I enjoy playing games and fetching sticks and balls, too.

I love being part of the family and don't like being left alone for long.

The Labrador retriever

Thick, tapering tail

Height:
54.5–57 cm

Weight:
25–34 kg

Colour:
yellow, black or
chocolate brown

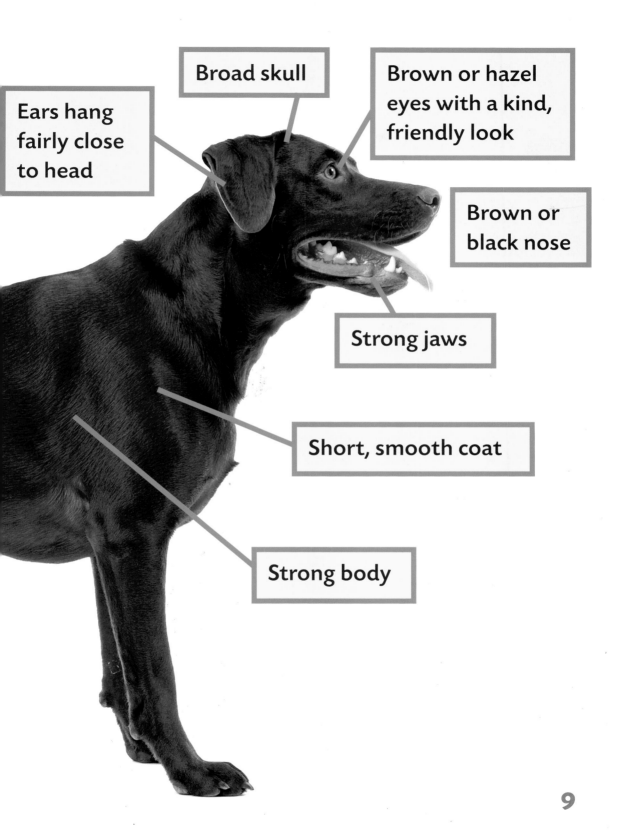

Broad skull

Brown or hazel eyes with a kind, friendly look

Ears hang fairly close to head

Brown or black nose

Strong jaws

Short, smooth coat

Strong body

9

All about Labradors

Labradors are from Newfoundland, Canada. They used to work with fishermen, helping to pull in nets and grab fish that tried to escape.

Some Labradors worked as sporting dogs, fetching catches for hunters.

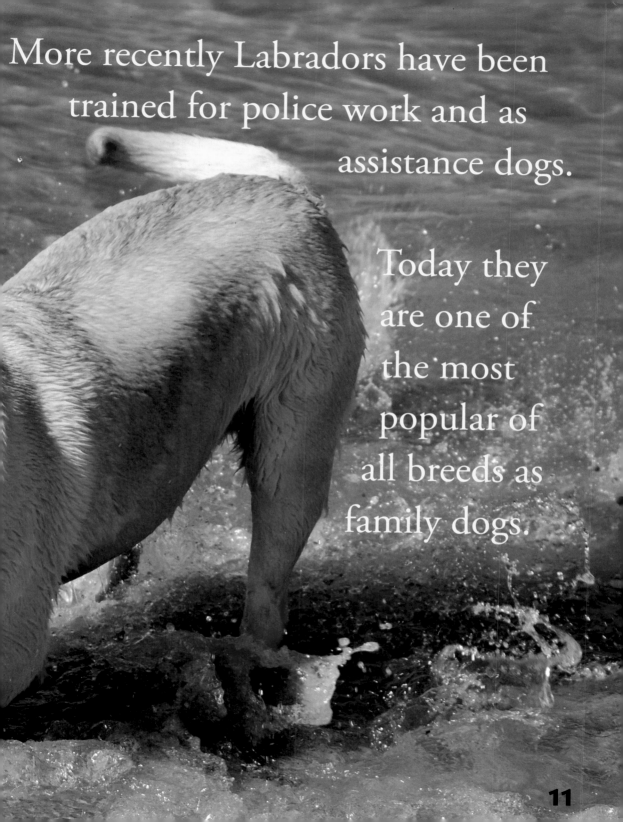

More recently Labradors have been trained for police work and as assistance dogs.

Today they are one of the most popular of all breeds as family dogs.

Growing up

Labrador puppies are very cute, but they grow into big dogs. Like all pups, Labradors should stay with mum for about eight weeks before going to a new home.

A Labrador misses her mum when she first goes to her new home.

Be extra kind and gentle with your little pup and she will soon learn to love her human family.

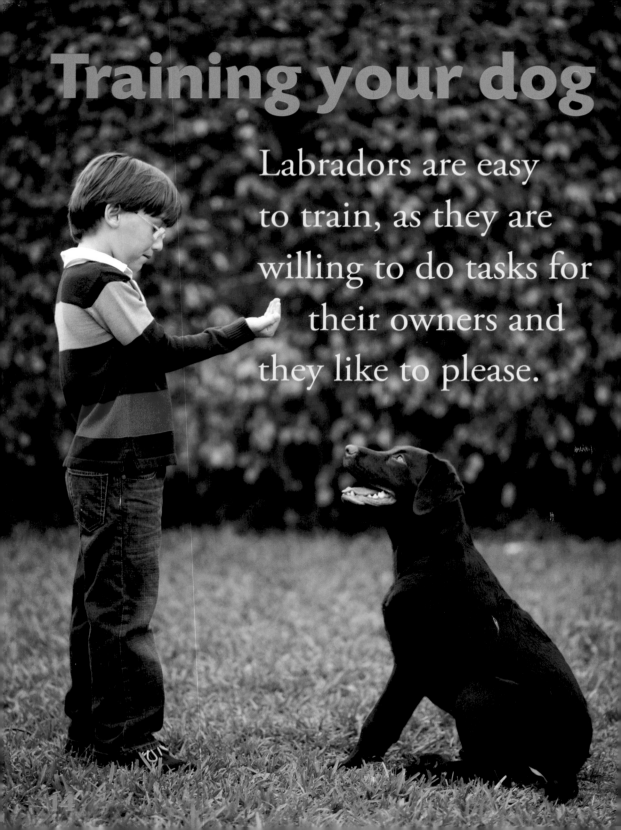

Training your dog

Labradors are easy to train, as they are willing to do tasks for their owners and they like to please.

It is important to train your Labrador when she's young and to show her that you are her pack leader.

Labradors can be trained to do important work, such as sniffing out forbidden items at airports.

Water dogs

Labradors love water and are always ready for a swim. The dog uses its thick tail to steer itself in water.

Webbing between the dog's toes helps it doggy-paddle fast.

A Labrador has a double coat.
The under layer keeps the dog warm,
and the outer
layer keeps out
water, so is
useful when
swimming.

Working dogs

Today, Labradors are very popular assistance dogs, helping people who are blind or have other disabilities.

These dogs are trustworthy, confident and hard working.

Not every pup is right for this work. Teaching an assistance dog

the skills it needs takes between 18 months and two years.

Your healthy dog

Your Labrador needs a good brush once a week to keep her coat in good condition. Only bathe her when she is really dirty. Check her teeth and make sure she gets used to you brushing them when she's a pup.

Have your pup checked before buying to make sure she will not have bone or joint problems. Labradors can have eye problems too.

Don't give your pup too much food; these dogs can easily become fat.

Caring for your dog

You and your family must think very carefully before buying a Labrador retriever. Remember, she may live as long as 11 years.

Every day your dog must have food, water and exercise, as well as lots of love and care. She will need to go to the vet for checks and vaccinations. When you and your family go out or away on holiday, she will have to be looked after.

Useful words

assistance dog
A dog that is specially trained to help people with disabilities or illnesses.

breed
A particular type of dog.

vaccinations
Injections given by the vet to protect your dog against certain illnesses.

Index

coat 9, 17, 20

ears 9
eyes 9, 21

food 21, 22

puppies 12, 13

swimming 16, 17

tail 8, 16
training 14, 15

walking 6
working dogs 10, 11, 15, 18, 19